Outdoor Designs
for Living

Michael Glassman

Photography by Amy Gallo

Schiffer Publishing Ltd

4880 Lower Valley Road Atglen, Pennsylvania 19310

Dedication

I dedicate this book to my sister Bonnie, without whose help, love, and support this book would never have been possible; and to my daughter Jordan, who is my greatest achievement. I love you both and you inspire me.

Schiffer Books are available at special discounts for bulk purchases for sales promotions or premiums. Special editions, including personalized covers, corporate imprints, and excerpts can be created in large quantities for special needs. For more information contact the publisher:

Published by Schiffer Publishing Ltd.
4880 Lower Valley Road
Atglen, PA 19310
Phone: (610) 593-1777; Fax: (610) 593-2002
E-mail: Info@schifferbooks.com

Other Schiffer Books on Related Subjects:
The Ultimate Wood-fired Oven Book. Anna Carpenter.
ISBN:978-0-7643-2916-6. $29.95

Bright Ideas: Sunrooms & Conservatories. Tina Skinner.
978-0-7643-1418-1. $29.95

For the largest selection of fine reference books on this and related subjects, please visit our web site at www.schifferbooks.com
We are always looking for people to write books on new and related subjects. If you have an idea for a book please contact us at the above address.

This book may be purchased from the publisher.
Include $5.00 for shipping.
Please try your bookstore first.
You may write for a free catalog.

In Europe, Schiffer books are distributed by
Bushwood Books
6 Marksbury Ave.
Kew Gardens
Surrey TW9 4JF England
Phone: 44 (0) 20 8392-8585; Fax: 44 (0) 20 8392-9876
E-mail: info@bushwoodbooks.co.uk
Website: www.bushwoodbooks.co.uk
Free postage in the U.K., Europe; air mail at cost.

Contents

To Ann
I hope this
inspires you
Enjoy Reading
Michael Glassman

Acknowledgments

I would like to thank all of the homeowners who graciously opened their homes for photography and gave me their support and inspiration.

My thanks goes to Amy Gallo, whose photography is wonderful and amazing. Working with you has been a joy. Thank you for your talent and friendship.

Thank you to Carla; your humor, friendship, and hard work makes our business enjoyable and a great reason to come to work each day.

To all the contractors: it is like building a town. My vision with your hard work and dedication makes these landscapes a beautiful reality.

And finally, to Matsudas of Sacramento: your plant material is amazing and it makes my vision much easier to accomplish.

Section 1:
Getting Started

Makeover frenzy is in. People love to redo the interiors of their homes. From magazines to televison and the Internet — everywhere you look, makeover possibilities abound. Every day we are told that by changing the decor of our homes we can improve our lives. People spend an inordinate amount of money on the interior of their houses, but what about the outside?

As a professional landscape designer for more than thirty years, I find that people budget huge amounts of money for the interiors of their homes but they tend to neglect the exteriors. I ask my clients all the time, does the interior of your home look better after seven to ten years, or is it just about time to redo everything? That amazing couch that you found in a trendy boutique in some exclusive resort — after

seven years, is it starting to look a bit shabby around the edges (and we're not talking chic either)?

On the flip side, at seven years of age a well-designed landscape has come into it's own and is really looking amazing. Shade trees have matured and now provide shade, ground cover has filled in, and there is no dirt to be seen. Patios have aged and now fit with the ambiance of the home.

So I ask you, which is truly the annuity, the shop-worn interior design that needs to be continually redone, or the exterior landscape that creates a whole new outdoor living environment while providing curb appeal and enhancing the value of your property.

Landscaping is your true annuity — it is the investment in your future.

A recent survey conducted by the American Household Furniture Alliance (AHFA) found that seventy percent of Americans wanted to spend more time outside and would like to create outdoor living spaces. Unfortunately, most people are unable to envision how to turn their plot of land into a usable outdoor environment.

This book is all about reclaiming lost outdoor spaces and transitioning from the inside to the outside. It provides readers with ideas on how to create outdoor rooms and includes a variety of before and after images to help them visualize the myriad of possibilities that can be created. Professionals will also find inspiration in this book, which provides specific examples of design details and solutions for their clients because good design is in the details.

Throughout my career I've developed a process for landscape design that is applicable for all size projects, from a tiny city courtyard to a palatial country estate. First and foremost, function is fundamental to the landscape design process. I mean by function that a space must work — walkways should be large enough to accommodate people, equipment, and even trashcans; while patios should be spacious enough to fit tables, chairs, chaises, and family members. No one has ever complained to me that they have too much entertainment space — an idea that has helped me to craft a philosophy on entertainment spaces that "bigger is better." However, with awareness of limited resources, function helps me to craft landscape designs that are ecologically sound and sustainable.

While function is foremost, aesthetics also is a primary concern in landscape design. If a site isn't beautiful, no one will want to use it. I tell my clients all the time that a big slab of concrete is functional, but if mud and weeds surround it, it's ugly and useless. Aesthetics include continuity of hardscape materials, carry-through of style from the interior to the exterior, and the appropriate use of planting materials. For example, it is important not to mix plants with different water requirements and/or different lighting needs – which means that sun plants require sun and shade plants need to be in the shade. Within the realm of aesthetics, it is important to develop a focal point to capture one's attention and create interest and drama in the landscape. An unusual piece of garden art, a spectacular fountain or water feature, and a dramatic plant or tree all can serve as important landscape focal points.

In addition to function and aesthetics, landscape designs must solve the specific problems that are indigenous to each site. Privacy concerns, water conservation, sound pollution, and poor drainage and erosion are just some of the issues that must be addressed in designing a landscape. If the unique site problems are not solved, issues of aesthetics and function are meaningless.

Throughout the sections in this book I address issues of function, aesthetics, and problem solving. For each section, I have included my top landscaping problems and solutions. The four sections of the book include: Getting Started; Front Yards; Back Yards; and Special Places, which includes Loggias, Pergolas and Gazebos, Poolscapes, Outdoor Kitchens, and Dining. I hope this book inspires you to step out and create an amazing outdoor living environment.

The Top Ten Landscaping Challenges

As a professional in the field, I do a lot of consulting and the following are the top ten landscaping problems I see every week. Throughout this book I include solutions to each of these challenges.

1) Privacy problems:
You've put in a huge pool and left no room to plant the trees you will need to block the view from your neighbor's two-story house; now you feel that you live in a fish bowl.

2) Mixing materials:
Your backyard is a hodgepodge of materials, colors, and textures. There's no harmony or continuity.

3) Improper layout of non-functional spaces:
You build your deck or patio without measuring your patio furniture and now it doesn't fit.

4) Separate modes of transportation:
No front walkway, so people have to squeeze past cars in the driveway to get to the front door.

5) The wrong plants in the wrong place:
You plant a fruitless mulberry for shade, too close to the house. Its invasive roots destroy the foundation and/or lawn. You have weeping willows with roots that get into the sewer system.

6) No building permits, improper setbacks, CC&Rs and easements:
Cities have certain building codes and restrictions that you need to know about and follow.

7) Improper mounding and the use of rocks and boulders:
Many times mounds look like dead horses are buried underneath them. Rocks and boulders not set properly look like meteors that dropped from the sky.

8) No focal point:
Like in any composition, a landscape needs a focal point to capture one's attention.

9) Sun plants in shade areas and visa-versa:
Plants that need less water are drowning next to plants that need a lot of water. Use plants with similar water and light requirements in the same area.

10) Lack of problem solving in the landscape:
Deer are eating the roses faster than you can grow them; the spa is poorly situated too far from the house; poor irrigation and drainage is destroying the landscape; street noise, barking dogs, and noisy neighbors make outdoor entertaining difficult. These challenges can be overcome.

Section 2:
Front Yards

"Little boxes on the hillside, little boxes made of ticky tacky. Little boxes on the hillside, little boxes all the same . There's a green one and a pink one and a blue one and a yellow one . And they're all made out of ticky tacky and they all look just the same" — Malvina Reynolds

Front yards in America have changed dramatically over the years. Until the twentieth century they were enclosed private spaces that grew flowers as well as edible and medicinal plants that were important for survival. These days in many places, front yards are indistinguishable from each other. Contemporary front yards usually consist of grass, trees, and plants along the foundation of the houses and they lack personality and style; they look like something out of the "Stepford Wives."

However, with skyrocketing land prices, smaller lot sizes, and water shortages homeowners are beginning to realize there are opportunities for creativity and sustainability; front yards don't need to look the same.

Front yards serve two somewhat contradictory functions: they not only connect us to the larger community but they also serve as buffers from the outside world. Front yards offer a first impression of what you're like. They reflect something about your style and personality, and can affect the value of your property.

This chapter showcases a variety of alternatives to the traditional front yard. It offers problem-solving solutions showcasing courtyards and private spaces. It also addresses new walkways that increase interest and curb appeal, and water conserving plantings that can replace the tired front lawn.

Helpful Hints For Front Yards

1) Whenever possible, separate your modes of transportation. Cars should use driveways and people should use separate front walkways.

2) Front walkways should be a minimum of five feet wide.

3) Try to avoid a straight front walkway so that it doesn't look like a tongue sticking out of someone's mouth. Stagger or curve the walkways to create more interest.

4) Try to use the same materials or color palate for both your indoors and outdoors. This will give you a greater continuity of design.

5) Consider raised planters, wing walls and different elevations to create greater curb appeal and interest.

6) If you have the space, think about creating an outdoor courtyard because it will give you more living space, create additional privacy and enhance the value of your house.

7) Consider the scale of your architecture when designing your front porch. In many respects, bigger is better and it will definitely help with the indoor/outdoor flow.

8) Curb appeal, curb appeal, curb appeal. Your front yard is the first impression of your house and the first impression of who you are.

9) Lawn is not the end all and be all of planting. We are conditioned to think that we must have a lawn in the front yard – this not true. Try to use plants with interesting color, texture and low water use.

10) A focal point adds additional drama and interest to your front yard. Fountains, architectural ornamentation, dramatic trees and plants or effective outdoor lighting are all examples of excellent focal points.

Traditional Elegance

BEFORE: This two-story Federal style home was built in a historic neighborhood in the 1920s. The existing walkway was straight and narrow and lead up to a small front porch. This house lacked curb appeal.

AFTER: We achieved greater curb appeal through a new random Peacock slate front walkway that encircled a raised front planter containing annual color and a specimen Japanese Maple (Acer palmatum 'Bloodgood'). We added black shutters to the windows and painted the trim of the house black.

BEFORE: The existing wood columns on the tiny front porch were rotting, the Crape Myrtle trees that flanked the front steps were misshapen and no longer bloomed and you could see the neighbors garbage cans from both sides of the driveway.

AFTER: We replaced the rotting wood columns with cast concrete stone columns in the same Doric style; we replaced the small brick and concrete porch with a larger slate porch and flanked the porch with raised planters containing three-tiered Alaska Azalea topiary trees.

The new larger slate porch encompassed the entire front of the house and provided seating space for the family. The raised planters offered elegance and drama to the front of the house and the rounded front steps assured much greater circulation and flow to the front porch as well as the front walkway.

We constructed a new wing wall at the end of the patio to block the view of the neighbors and their garbage cans. The wall was built from CMU (concrete masonry unit) concrete block and was faced with house plaster and a slate border. To create a focal point in the center of the wall, we installed a custom designed marble wall fountain. The fountain helped to mask street noise. CLK Construction was the building contractor for this project.

Suburban Sustainability

BEFORE: This 1950s suburban tract home was the epitome of urban blight with its rotting wood planter, dying front lawn and clipped blob hedges. It had absolutely no curb appeal.

AFTER: We removed the old planters, the lawn and hedges, painted the house a sage green color and went for a colorful, low-maintenance, low-water plant palate.

BEFORE: The existing Cherry tree was dead, the shrubs were overgrown and the front of the house had no privacy. The property contained one nice specimen Kumquat tree.

AFTER: We achieved privacy by constructing a new courtyard.

15

BEFORE: Home owners looked out to a
dead tree and busy suburban street.

AFTER: The new courtyard included antique iron grates that softened a blank wall, a wonderful copper
and concrete noise-reducing fountain, colorful pots and limestone tile paving.

The new drought tolerant, low maintenance plantings incorporated the client's aloe collection as well as variegated New Zealand flax (Phormium tenax), Spanish lavender (Lavandula stoechas), blue fescue grass (Festuca glauca), orange day lilies (Hemerocallis), multi-stem crape myrtle trees (Lagerstroemia indica) and ornamental strawberry ground cover (Fragaria). As a banding along the foundation of the house, we also incorporated the client's decorative rock collection, which provided additional drainage and kept water away from the foundation.

Wonderful custom wrought iron gates lead into the new courtyard flanked by CMU concrete block, faced with stucco painted the house color and capped with a limestone facia. A decorative antique window was incorporated into both of the walls to add drama as well as air flow. The fountain was flanked by a vertical growing horsetail (Equisetum), which enhanced the drama of the fountain. Construction by Matt Hazeltine Landscaping.

BEFORE: This 1940s cottage had many problems. There was no porch or railing on the steps, the front walkway was too narrow and the front of the house had no charm.

Wing walls were installed flanking the new front slate landing and slate steps. We planted spiral junipers (Juniperus chinensis 'Sea Green spirals') to punctuate the front entry and lined the front walkway with a boxwood hedge (Buxus japonica).

AFTER: We painted the orange brick and planted creeping fig (Ficus pumila) to grow over the front walls. We installed a new black and leaded glass front door along with black shutters, which flanked the windows. We also enlarged the front walkway and overlaid it with autumn slate twelve-inch tiles.

A decorative two-tiered fountain was centered in the front window; an iron arch planted with potato vine (Solanum) was positioned over the fountain and Chinese fringe flowers (Loropetalum) flanked either side of the fountain.

Contemporary Eclectic

BEFORE: This contemporary house is dull; the front lawn requires too much water and the front of the house has no curb appeal. The landscape does not enhance the architecture of the house.

AFTER: We played off the architectural details of the house by creating different levels. We used wing walls and raised planters, constructed of CMU block, faced with hand troweled plaster capped with ceramic tile end installed low voltage eyeball lights to illuminate the architectural details.

We constructed a new stair-stepped walkway out of concrete faced with the same ceramic tile that was used in the inside of the house. We used plants with very distinct shapes to create living pieces of art. For example, in the front planter we used a Bonsai black pine (Pinus thunbergii) and next to the fountain we chose a weeping serpentine cedar (Cedrus atlantica 'glauca pendula'). The remaining plants were drought-tolerant with interesting foliage and shapes.

We installed a twelve foot monolithic stone fountain as a focal point. We used horsetails (Equisetum hyemale) and papyrus (Cyperus) to soften the vertical character of the fountain.

BEFORE: This home required people to enter from the driveway and the house lacked curb appeal.

AFTER: The front portico entry had interesting Boquet Canyon flagstone on the columns that we played off of for the front yard design. We constructed a new front walkway flanked with two raised planters, constructed out of concrete block, faced and caped with the Boquet Canyon stone. We installed white standard Natchez crape myrtle trees (Lagerstroemia indica 'Natchez') in each of the planters. To create privacy, we installed three-foot high raised planters, also faced in the stone to create the feel of a courtyard.

BEFORE: The large sloping front lawn, on a corner lot, was a water hog and the living room had no privacy.

AFTER: We installed a new stamped concrete driveway in the same color scheme as the flagstone and separated the driveway from the separate front walkway with a raised planter. We planted free-form topiary juniper (Juniperus chinensis 'Sea Green freeform') and pigmy dwarf barberry shrubs (Berberis 'Crimson Pygmy').

Opposite page:
Black bamboo (Phyllostachys nigra) provided a living privacy screen that allowed the light and the air to filter through. Custom wrought-iron gates provided additional security and enclosed the courtyard and a magnificent Asian bust becomes the focal point as water cascades off its face. The fountain is surrounded with Chinese fringe flowers (Loropetalum). Construction by Green Futures Landscaping.

Hillside Elegance

BEFORE: Elegant Mediterranean home on a hill had no separate front walkway and the hillside was a miss-mash of different plant types.

AFTER: We unified the planting with a variety of color including white iceberg roses (Rosa 'iceberg'), red carpet roses (Rosa 'flora carpet), dwarf Manzanita ground cover (Arctostaphylos 'Emerald carpet') and we stabilized the hillside and added color and interest.

BEFORE: This custom house looked unfinished and had no curb appeal.

AFTER: A dramatic new stairway constructed of poured concrete faced with travertine tiles and flanked with stair stepped wing walls along with low-voltage lighting and architectural caste-iron pots created a dramatic entry to this house.

Right:
We saw-cut the existing driveway and installed travertine tiles and new front steps to create additional continuity. Spiral junipers (Juniperus chinensis 'Sea Green spirals') and white iceberg roses (Rosa 'iceberg') softened the foundation of the house while gaura (Gaura lindheimeri) and red carpet roses (Rosa 'flora carpet') created color and interest on the hillside. A custom arched gate separates the back yard from the front yard.

We decided to build a private courtyard off the kitchen and breakfast eating area of this brand new custom home. The outer walls were surrounded with a raised planter, constructed CMU block, capped with two-inch bull-nosed limestone and faced with hand-troweled plaster and Tunisian tile accent. We planted lavender (Lavandula dentata), bougainvillea vines (Bougainvillea 'Barbara Karst') and dark pink carpet roses (Rosa flora carpet).

The focal point of the courtyard was a ceramic pot fountain; the basin that the water flowed into was faced in Tunisian tiles. The flooring of the courtyard was French limestone and we inset antique iron grates into the block walls to provide openness and light and to allow the breezes to flow through.

Shady Retreat

When you're faced with the problem of deep shade, a traditional grass lawn doesn't work. Grass requires full sun. The solution is to use shade-loving perennials and shrubs such as Japanese maples (Acer palmatum 'Bloodgood'), azaleas, impatiens, ferns and dwarf boxwoods (Buxus 'suffruticosa'). A beautiful random quartzite walkway and patio doesn't have to be watered and thrives in deep shade.

A beautiful carved limestone fountain, surrounded by impatiens, creates a great focal point for the front yard. Indigenous boulders can be softened by hydrangeas (Hydrangea macrophylla) and carpet roses (Rosa flora carpet).

It is the attention to details that truly solves design problems and makes a landscape unique. Fountains make a wonderful focal point and help alleviate noise pollution.

Wrought-iron gates and antique window grates allow light and air to circulate while still providing privacy and adding a touch of elegance.

When using pots or urns on pedestals be sure to include drip irrigation through the bottom of the pots and also to install area drains underneath the pots so that the water does not leak out and stain the pedestals. Trailing perennials can soften the hardness of the pots.

Left:
This is a nice solution to mixing materials using brick and similar colored random slate.

Right:
A creative solution to capping masonry block walls using bull-nosed ceramic tile for the cap and the reveal.

A decorative square lattice fence planted with a flowering vine blocks out the view of an air conditioner and ugly pool equipment.

Using the client's decorative stone collection makes for a creative solution to a drainage problem. Under the stone is landscape fabric with a French drain, which keeps the water off of the foundation of the house.

Planting materials are the epitome of design in the details. Perennials (pictured) such as aloes with Spanish lavender (Lavandula stoechas), foxglove (Digitalis), white iceberg roses and red carpet roses soften and otherwise hard landscape.

Section 3:
Back Yards

"If you can't find what you're looking for in your own backyard, maybe you never really lost it at all." —Dorothy Gale from *The Wizard of Oz*

With the development of suburbs after World War II, back yards became cornerstones of outdoor entertaining. For the first time, many homeowners had enclosed private spaces where they could cook and visit with their family and friends away from the noise and traffic of the city.

The word "yard" is derived from the Middle English term "yerd," which means "enclosure." The concept of a yard has evolved from an enclosed outdoor space to the creation of an outdoor room.

Today's outdoor rooms have extended the usability of the home — with fireplaces, heaters, misters, and fans; back yard spaces can be used throughout the day and night and in all seasons of the year. In addition to gardening, people now cook and eat outside, watch movies and television, dance and exercise in their newly created outdoor environments.

The hardscapes and softscapes of back yard landscape design are addressed in this chapter. Hardscapes are the walks, decks, patios, and other permanent features; while softscapes include plant materials, mulches, and soils. The chapter also addresses a variety of problems related to outdoor entertaining. Issues of privacy, noise pollution, drainage and erosion, spatial relations, and an overall unification of the house with the garden are explored, as well as major landscaping *faux pas*.

The Top Ten Landscaping Tips To Remember

Houses are built to live in, and not to look on: therefore let use be preferred before uniformity. – Francis Bacon, 17th century

1) Think about large gardens in terms of feet. Small gardens are so attentive to detail you must learn to think about space and plants in mere inches.

2) You must design every inch of the garden; if you neglect a corner or leave something out, it will bug you forever.

3) The priority is to make spaces for people, not plants. Once people are served, then you may embellish with plants.

4) To enhance the indoor-outdoor connections, pay attention to how the garden is viewed from indoors through major windows and doors. Position the focal points to respond to these views.

5) Small gardens do not often have views outside their limits. Carefully chosen garden art is the best way to provide something to look at while you are living and dining outdoors.

6) Nothing animates a landscape better than a water feature. The glistening drops and sound of falling water not only masks city noise, it elicits a primal response in the brain that has a calming effect on the body.

7) Small gardens use very little paving. This greatly reduces your construction costs leaving more in the budget to explore high quality tactile materials such as stone or tile. When viewed so closely, these materials in paving, walls and other constructed elements will prove an elegant and interesting way to unify the site.

8) Building walls and fences are formidable enclosures that make the space seem smaller than it actually is. Downplay their oppressive height with techniques such as espaliers, clinging vines, draped flowering vines, friezes, and contrasting trellage.

9) Utilize plants that are in scale with the space. Choose small herbaceous perennials and dwarf shrubs, with very small trees that flower or turn color in fall. These will never outgrow their space. Avoid larger woody shrubs and shade trees.

10) Plant small landscapes with plenty of diversity so there is a broad range of color and texture throughout the garden. It is easy when space is limited to succumb to a monotonous palate that fails to provide adequate interest.

Contemporary Chic

BEFORE: This outdated 1940s house and garden offered a boring slab of concrete which bore no relationship to the house. There was no separation between the patio, driveway and garage and no easy access to the back patio.

AFTER: We designed an elevated Quartzite patio which created the ultimate outdoor room. New doors from both the kitchen and the dining room allow guests to circulate to the new outdoor environment. Stucco walls separate the elevated patio from the driveway and the garage and create a more intimate space.

BEFORE: A large water-loving lawn is high maintenance and boring. A lone palm tree sat in the back corner with decaying wood fences that were falling down.

AFTER: The decaying wood fences were replaced with contemporary stucco walls and a rectangular pool with arching side jets and a rear sheer descent created drama and interest and transformed the backyard from a passive space to an interactive area. The lower patio is a great space for chaise lounges and additional dining.

This upper terrace is equipped with a contemporary gas fire place and an outdoor kitchen. Cable railing enclosed the space yet allows maximum views, while comfortable furniture truly makes the space the ultimate outdoor room.

Traditional Elegance

BEFORE: This 1920s home has doors that opened onto the backyard then stepped down to a disjointed brick patio. There was no privacy from the neighbors and the existing fence was falling down. The owners wanted a backyard with maximum entertainment space.

AFTER: An upper terrace at the same elevation as the doors was constructed with Peacock slate tiles and created a large entertainment space. Additional seating was provided by the new seat walls, which flanked the new terrace and were constructed with CMU block, faced in random slate and caped with a poured concrete cap.

BEFORE: An outdated gazebo at the end of the pool was ugly and devoid of any elegance. The perimeter fence was unattractive and falling down. Dying shrubs blocked the view of the pool from the gazebo and the gazebo was structurally unsound and lacked lighting or fans.

AFTER: The new gazebo was ideal for entertaining. A custom gas fireplace provides warmth during the evenings. The vaulted solid overhead was equipped with fans, low-voltage lighting and gas heaters. Comfortable furniture made this truly an outdoor room. Italian Cypress (Cupressus sempervirens) was planted behind the gazebo to create an evergreen screen to block out the neighbors.

46

BEFORE: The existing pool was a boring rectangle with no focal point. The space around the pool was broken up with an unusable lawn and the back of the pool provided no privacy from the neighbors.

AFTER: We demolished the old pool and constructed a new pool with a beautiful wall fountain which flows into the elevated spa. The spa then flows into the pool. The wall fountain was flanked with a columnade planted with star Jasmine (Trachelospermum jasminoides), which creates a wonderful focal point and provides an interesting change of elevation for the pool. Random Peacock slate patios flanked the pool and a raised planter constructed of CMU block, faced with random slate was planted with Italian Cypress (Cupressus sempervirens). The Cypress provided elegance and privacy along with a new Boxwood hedge (Buxus japonica).

A covered loggia flanked part of the upper terrace and led to the lower outdoor kitchen complete with a pizza oven, BBQ, warming drawer, refrigerator and sink. The loggia was equipped with built-in gas heaters, misters, fans, low-voltage lighting and speakers.

The upper terrace creates a more formal elegant outdoor room for entertaining. We also designed a channel drain to eliminate drainage problems. A fifty-year-old Bonsai black pine (Pinus thunbergii) creates a focal point and creates a living piece of art.

Cast concrete ballastrades and columns reinforce the architectural integrity of the design. Low voltage lighting creates safety and ambiance and the back wall fountain and the pool tile are made of antique marble and truly add to the overall beauty. Construction by CLK Construction.

Woodland Farmhouse

BEFORE: The rustic farmhouse lacked focus, function and form. The plantings were sparse, the brick fireplace stuck out and the gravel walkway was too narrow and too close to the foundation of the house.

AFTER: The new slate walkway softened the generous foundation plantings consisting of dwarf boxwood (Buxus 'suffruticosa'), azaleas, bulbs and dwarf gardenias (Gardenia radicans).

BEFORE: The square rear deck was rotting and appeared to be stuck onto the back of the house. It housed an assortment of undesirable wild animals including snakes, rats and skunks. The large boulder, which was used as a seat by the grandchildren, had been dumped in a muddy area

AFTER: The square deck was replaced with an elevated brick patio, equipped with a raised planter and a beautiful brick fireplace. The seating boulder was surrounded by a spacious lawn, which is now used for croquet, volleyball and other outdoor sports.

BEFORE: An upstairs game room over the garage leads to a small wood landing and ugly stairs. Although the game room has one of the best views, there was no usable entertainment space.

AFTER: A large twenty foot by twenty foot upper slate patio supported by square brick columns created a beautiful outdoor room off of the upstairs game room. Under the new patio became a great space for the ultimate outdoor kitchen.

An elegant spiral iron staircase, with slate risers and treads leads from the upper patio to the lower entertainment spaces.

In the lower patio, a custom fountain created a focal point and helps to eliminate the surrounding street noise.

This outdoor kitchen was equipped with black granite countertops, stainless steel BBQ, sink, dishwasher, warming drawer, fans, heaters and misters. We faced the back wall of the kitchen with the same brick as the house creating additional architectural cohesiveness.

A three-tiered spa was built to add to the ultimate entertainment quotient of the property. Again we used brick that matched the house for all of the vertical structures including planters and walls. All of the paving was constructed out of Autumn flagstone which complimented the brick and provided a contrast.

The property has magnificent views of both a natural forest, which we under planted with spring bulbs, as well as the neighboring hills and skyline. Contracting was completed by Empire Construction.

Asian Influence

BEFORE: This tract home had a disjointed aggregate and brick patio. The patio was exposed to the hot afternoon sun and the landscape had no distinguishable style.

AFTER: We replaced the old patio with a Boquet Canyon flagstone patio that matched the stone on the front of the house. A beautiful overhead structure, with stone columns, shielded the patio from the hot afternoon sun. An outdoor fan deters bugs and keeps the patio cooler.

BEFORE: The back of the house was nondescript. A raised planter in front of the sliding door blocked circulation and created a bottleneck at one end of the patio.

AFTER: The new extensive patio provided more usable space and created more of an outdoor room.

The asymmetric custom gas fireplace, flanked with seat walls and a curved hearth were all faced in Boquet Canyon flagstone, which created an intimate space for outdoor enjoyment. Red Dragon Japanese Maples (Acer palmatum dissectum 'Red Dragon') soften the stone and add drama to the landscape.

We designed an outdoor kitchen at the opposite end of the patio. A curving granite-topped counter created a great conversation area to congregate and visit with the chef.

A retaining wall of natural boulders holds back the hillside. Japanese painted ferns (Athyrium niponicum), autumn ferns (Dryopteris erythrosora) and a stone lantern add interest to the sloping hillside.

A large grass area created an open space or vista from the patio. A contemporary monolithic fountain provided a focal point for the yard. The fountain was placed in a raised planter and surrounded with Society Garlic (Tulbaghia).

A hammock set amongst a backdrop of timber bamboo (Bambusa oldhamii) and Evergreen Pear trees (Prunus kawakamii) provides a wonderful respite from a stressful lifestyle. Construction by Green Future.

A side yard is not a throw away space. A four-foot wide, stamped concrete walkway, leads you to your eventual destination. We planted black bamboo (Phyllostachys nigra) for additional privacy. Mondo Grass (Ophiopogon) served as a border in front of the bamboo.

Contemporary Living Art

BEFORE: The neighbor's two story house creates a privacy problem for this dated landscape. The wood overhead, fence, aggregate and brick patio and lawn area does not create a feeling of an outdoor room.

AFTER: We installed clumping timber bamboo (Bambusa oldhamii) to create privacy. Dylan Tellesen and Robin Indar created handmade mosaic tiles that were used to construct the new pool, spa and fireplace. Ultimately a new contemporary outdoor space was created.

A cobalt blue pot fountain created a wonderful focal point for the side yard.

Bottom left:
The evergreen clumping timber bamboo (Bambusa oldhamii) grows to thirty-five feet, and provides great screening. For additional interest, fountain grass (Pennisetum) was planted in front of the bamboo.

Bottom right:
Handmade mosaic tiles add drama and interest to the pool and spa walls.

BEFORE: The back of the house had a large step down from the back door to the lower concrete slab. A wrought iron fence made the space feel like a prison.

AFTER: We designed an upper terrace at the same elevation as the back door which made the new stamped concrete patio feel more like a room. Under the kitchen window, a serving counter with a granite counter top was a great space for serving food. A three-inch channel drain provided drainage for the upper terrace.

BEFORE: The back of the house was ugly. The upper balcony stuck out from the second story and there was no entertainment space.

AFTER: A heavy duty pergola structure made of large timbers was constructed over the upper terrace. It created shade and gave the terrace the feel of a room. Stone-faced seat walls with travertine capping provided a break between the terrace and the pool.

BEFORE: An outdated free-formed pool surrounded by cracked concreted and an old fence was dated. There was no privacy. This back yard had no focal point, no color, no style and no class.

AFTER: Along the pool, we designed a two-tiered raised planter, faced in stone and capped in travertine. Large standard Photinia trees (Photinia Fraseri std.) were planted to provide privacy and block the neighbor's view. The pool was retiled and replastered and new stamped concrete matching the stone was installed.

A magnificent arched wall fountain was placed in the raised planter. Tear drop Juniper topiary ((Juniperus chinensis 'Sea Green tear drop) flanked the fountain with white iceberg roses (Rosa iceberg) and white carpet roses (Rosa flora carpet) inside the raised planter. This truly provided a great focal point and masked the sound of the neighbors.

Below, left and right:
A beautiful stone faced gas fireplace, with a heavy timbered wood mantle, created privacy on the upper terrace. On either side of the fireplace we planted long leafed yellow wood (Podocarpus henkelii) to give additional screening. Landscape contracting by Empire Construction.

Miami Deco

BEFORE: This house had a very narrow backyard devoid of color and interest with limited space. The client wanted a pool or spa or a fountain with lots of color and usable space.

AFTER: A unique outdoor room. The old concrete was covered with desert gold quartzite tile, a dramatic fire bowl was installed on top of a granite slab shelf, the square stucco columns were faced with pre-cast concrete to match the inside of the residence and new colorful and comfortable furniture was added.

BEFORE: A small patch of lawn was a waste of space and used too much water. The concrete was boring and the space was too open.

AFTER: The lawn was removed and replaced with a new quartzite patio. A rough wood pergola with cast concrete columns was installed. The focal point was a gas fireplace flanked by topiary three-tiered privets (Ligustrum japonicum). A retractable shade eliminated the late afternoon sun.

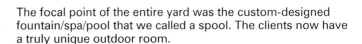

The pergola was stained walnut color and covered with a shade cloth to reduce the heat load without loosing too much natural light. A chandelier provides light and elegance to the space. Sago Palms (Cycas revoluta) were planted in large coral glazed pots to add color and interest.

The focal point of the entire yard was the custom-designed fountain/spa/pool that we called a spool. The clients now have a truly unique outdoor room.

BEFORE: This side yard was a throw away space – it offered no privacy from the neighbors and the air conditioner units were exposed.

AFTER: We designed a comfortable four foot wide travertine tile walkway. The fence and house walls were softened with Italian Cypress (Cupressus sempervirens), Japanese maples (Acer palmatum) and flax (Phormium tenax).

A custom outdoor shower faced in travertine tile is a great amenity to have before taking a swim. Potato vines (Solanum rantonnetii) flanked the outdoor shower.

Travertine steps and retaining walls provide access to the top of the hillside. Red carpet roses (Rosa flora carpet) trail over the walls and green spiral Junipers (Juniperus chinensis 'Sea Green spirals') punctuate the staircase entrance.

Right:
BEFORE: Keystone block terraced the bare hillside. The existing backyard was bare dirt and drainage was a major problem that needed to be addressed.

Far right:
AFTER: New concrete block retaining walls faced and capped in travertine tile were

installed. French drains were installed behind each of the walls. A dramatic stair-stepped waterfall traverses down the hillside and flows into the new swimming pool.

Trailing Rosemary (Rosmarinus officinalis) flow over the walls. Pink iceberg roses (Rosa iceberg), Red carpet roses (Rosa flora carpet) and tear drop Junipers (Juniperus chinensis 'Sea Green tear drops) add color and interest to the hillside.

Above and right:
The hillside elegance and pool enhance the dramatic architecture of the residence. At the top of the water staircase, the client's Winged Victory statue was showcased.

A tile patio flanks the dramatic pool and provides ample seating and dining areas. A cast concrete gas fireplace and a prefabricated outdoor kitchen provide interest and make this space feel like an extension of the house.

BEFORE: The existing patio was an unattractive gray concrete and was exposed to the afternoon sun. The patio was too small and there were too many potted plants and blank walls.

AFTER: The new patio was expanded and covered with large terra cotta tiles. A steel pergola overhead structure with outdoor fans was installed. A beautiful wall fountain with flowering vines now gives interest to a once boring wall.

BEFORE: Concrete walls originally chopped up the patio and produced a non-usable alley way behind the wall.

AFTER: We removed the walls and expanded the patio at the same level, making the space feel more like an outdoor room.

BEFORE: The low hedge closed in the existing yard. The clients wanted a pool and more entertainment space and the yard needed a dramatic focal point.

AFTER: The new pool created a visual vista and provided additional entertainment opportunities.

BEFORE: The expansive lawn was never used. It required too much maintenance and too much water. This area of the landscape was going to waste.

AFTER: The pool with arching jets provided a new sense of purpose for the landscape. The clients felt they were vacationing in their own backyard. The terra cotta paving unified the entertainment space making all areas flow together.

The new custom outdoor kitchen provided seating on the upper patio as well as a functional and usable space for the pool area. The kitchen included a BBQ, burners, double warming drawers, refrigerator, storage and a sink.

The classic-shaped pool was designed with arching deck jets, a ground level curved spa and a beautiful raised-tile fountain flanked with raised planters planted with boxwoods (Buxus 'suffruticosa') and annual color. This pool was truly a visual treat.

Amenities such as custom towels, robes and slippers makes you feel like you are vacationing at a resort.

The ultimate outdoor dining experience: a custom gas fireplace, an elegant table setting and comfortable furniture around the fire. Contracting by CLK construction.

Mediterranean Estate

Photos by Dave Henry, Davehenryphoto.com

This covered logia creates a true indoor-outdoor experience. French limestone paving and rough wood beams flow from the inside of the house to the outside. The custom outdoor gas fireplace provides warmth and a wonderful seating area. Photo by Dave Henry.

This outdoor eating area is both spacious and elegant. Fans and recessed lighting complete this dramatic outdoor room. Photos by Dave Henry.

Below:
The custom designed pool includes a raised sheeting spa, French limestone paving and coping and raised planters constructed of CMU block, hand troweled plaster with four by four decorative Tunisian tile insets.

The pool house design included space for storage, pool equipment and an outdoor shower. We designed the ultimate custom wall fountain with cobalt blue glass tiles and Tunisian tile insets. A Tunisian tile mural was inset into a niche on the other side of the pool house.

BEFORE: This narrow suburban backyard had privacy problems. The yard also had a major drainage problem and the clients wanted a tropical outdoor paradise.

IN PROGRESS: The pool we designed started to create interest but the lack of privacy and non-usable space still needed to be addressed.

AFTER: The new environment is the epitome of the ultimate outdoor room. Fabric covered gazebos with hanging chandeliers, a travertine-faced gas fireplace and comfortable furniture make this a wonderful space.

AFTER: Raised planters surround the patio area. The planters were built of CMU block faced and capped in travertine tile and included French drains. We planted evergreen Photinia trees (Photinia fraseri std.) for privacy, flax (Phormium tenax) and Queen palms (Syagrus romanzoffianum) for drama.

Two fabric covered gazebos were installed – one was for dining and the other was for lounging in front of the fire. The dining gazebo was adjacent to the custom outdoor kitchen.

Because the yard was narrow, I designed a pool that wrapped around the corner. This way I could maximize both the pool size and the usable entertainment space. Sheer descent fountain spillways create interest and mask the sound of neighboring houses.

Joseph's Coat climbing roses soften the house foundation. Channel drains provide additional drainage for the colored concrete patio and the evergreen plantings block the view of the neighbors' homes.

A custom Travertine faced outdoor kitchen makes this retreat the ultimate for outdoor dining.

English Tudor

BEFORE: The pool was too close to the residence. A temporary fence kept the children from falling in the pool but made the place feel like a prison.

AFTER: The pool was filled in to accommodate a new entertainment space. The existing window at the back of the house was converted into a French door and a large elevated outdoor loggia was constructed.

BEFORE: A tall privet hedge enclosed the area off the pool and blocked the expansive view of the property.

AFTER: The hedge was removed an a new elevated patio and outdoor kitchen was installed which took advantage of the magnificent view.

91

The new entertainment loggia was designed to emulate the architecture of the residence. Features included gas heaters, outdoor fans, chandelier lighting, a magnificent custom gas fireplace, outdoor kitchen as well as a built-in movie screen and projector. This is the epitome of outdoor living at its finest.

The new swimming pool includes an automated cover which eliminates the fear of children falling in. the pool has an infinity edge, brick coping and beautiful random slate paving.

A new raised planter includes a boxwood hedge (Buxus 'suffruticosa'), feather grass (Stipa), standard Wisteria trees (Wisteria sinesis std.) and white trailing Lantana (Lantana montevidensis).

I designed the ultimate children's space complete with a play structure with rubber mulch, an incredible fountain with spray jets and no standing water, a whimsical outdoor gazebo and a checker board synthetic grass and brick paving. Even the iron pots were planted with edible grapes and purple fountain grass (Pennesitum rubra). Contracting by CLK Construction.

Modern Rustica

BEFORE: The contemporary home on a large piece of property lacked adequate entertainment space. The existing retaining walls were stark and the client had problems with voles (a cross between a mole and a gopher).

AFTER: We solved the vole problem by constructing raised planter walls made out of CMU faced with plaster with a cast concrete cap broken up with large granite boulders. The soil was removed two feet below the planter walls and heavy wire mesh was installed along the bottom of the planters before adding new topsoil. The wire mesh inhibited the voles from digging into the planters.

BEFORE: The back wall of the pool was ugly and was stained with calcium deposits.

AFTER: The back wall was faced with glass tiles and a lower planter was constructed which softened the one time stark wall.

BEFORE: Weeds and clover covered the lower area below the upper terrace.

AFTER: Large squares of acid-stained concrete provided a new expansive entertainment area for dining, lounging and large parties.

A curved planter filled with Euphorbia, Barberry (Berberis 'Crimson Pygmy') and rush grass (Juncus) encircle a lower fire pit. Rusted iron giraffes surrounded by Lavender (Lavandula stoechas) add whimsy to the landscape and look as if they're grazing on the prairie. Installation by Cathy D's in Grass Valley.

The renovated pool and lower patio created a wonderful focal point and a great outdoor room. A lower seat wall created intimacy on the lower patio.

A garden takes on an entirely new environment at night. Low voltage lighting can add safety to steps, drama to seat walls, accent a fountain, highlight a structure and add drama to surrounding plantings.

Sometimes lighting fixtures can also enhance the garden and reinforce the landscape theme.

When addressing a blank
wall, there are several creative
solutions. An arched trellis planted
with a flowering vine or a tile
mosaic can add interest. A series
of mirrors on a garden fence can
reflect the surrounding landscape
and create depth.

This beautiful spiral iron staircase with slate treads is a great problem solver from the upper level to the ground.

Art in the garden. These two sculptures add drama and create a focal point for the landscape. Sculptures by Curt Stiger (grass Valley).

Rain chains serve as an artistic solution to draining the roofline of a structure. Cable railing provides security while still allowing you to see the view below.

A custom iron gate adds whimsy and interest.

This granite boulder breaks up the hard lines of the planter and seat wall.

A travertine faced pedestal with a dramatic pot and low voltage lighting add interest to the planter wall.

Section 4:
Special Places

"There are places I remember all my life, Though some have changed, Some forever, not for better, Some have gone and some remain. All these places have their moments, of lovers and friends I still can recall, some are dead and some are living. In my life I've loved them all." —The Beatles, *In my Life*

Whether it is an area where you can retreat, a place to read or meditate, a space for children to play, or a liquid escape, a place to swim, spa, lounge, or soak up the sun, there are places in a garden that are special. Maybe it's a place to cook and dine *alfresco*, or a chance to sit by the fire and gaze at the stars on a cold evening that fulfills all your dreams. These are the special places, the environments that are not traditionally found in the front or back yard but that we are equally drawn to. Step into these magical places and enjoy them.

Hints For Designing Your Outdoor Kitchen

1) For an outdoor kitchen, think in terms of how you would plan for the indoors.

2) Make sure you have enough space to work. Consider the possible amenities and decide what's most important to include. Do you want a warming drawer? A BBQ? An oven? A refrigerator is one of the nicest things to have. If you can locate the sewer line, you can include hot and cold running water and even an outdoor dishwasher.

3) Design an area where people can sit and talk to you while you cook. Be sure to design the space so that you face your company – that way everyone can hang out and enjoy each other.

4) Try to use some of the same materials in your outdoor kitchen as you do in your inside. This will create continuity between the indoors and outdoors.

5) Be sure to provide shade, in the form of an umbrella or a trellis. If you opt for a trellis, include electrical power so that you can run an outdoor fan to discourage bugs.

The Ultimate Outdoor Kitchen

A photo gallery of unique outdoor kitchens.

A Special Children's Retreat

This whimsical fenced children's play area includes a fountain with arching jets, a beautiful red gazebo, a climbing structure with swings, slides and ropes and a checkerboard of synthetic grass and brick. A center drain captures the water and recycles it.

This beautiful rose garden, with raised brick planters and climbing rose arches, creates a truly special place.

The raised vegetable planters, built from concrete block faced and capped with real stone, adds a sense of elegance to this vegetable garden.

This exterior atrium was designed as a place of worship for a synagogue. I designed the space to have the feeling of old Jerusalem using natural stone columns and hand-chiseled stone blocks.

This wine cellar was designed with an arched vaulted brick ceiling and a flagstone floor to emulate an underground grotto, perfect for an intimate dinner and wine tasting.

This gallery of custom designed fountains and water features adds drama and focus and creates a special atmosphere to each place.

This romantic white gazebo is a special place to sit and relax while enjoying the beauty of the surrounding rose garden.

112

This three-tiered custom spa creates a special environment.

This portable spa was designed to feel built-in. It was placed near the master bedroom and flanked with spiral junipers (Juniperus chinensis 'Sea Green spirals') and a square lattice screen, planted with white clematis.

Each of these custom designed pools provide a liquid escape – a place to relax, swim and take respite from the hot summer sun. These poolscapes are indeed very special places.

Many clients need inspiration for design. Often they simply want to look at examples of fireplaces in order to decide what amenities they would like to include. The following is a photo gallery of outdoor gas fireplaces. My hope is that the variation of styles provides inspiration. Enjoy.

BEFORE: This space lacked privacy and the concrete was disjointed. The area had no focus.

AFTER: The new private outdoor kitchen created an outdoor dining environment.

BEFORE: An ugly garage door and an unpainted wood pergola made for an outdated and unusable space.

AFTER: The old garage door was replaced with a custom carriage door which made the space feel more like a guest house. A new custom outdoor kitchen with a ledge stone veneered cabinet and a granite slab countertop made this a wonderful outdoor kitchen

The overhead structure created shade while the serving counter, with bar stools, offered a great conversation area.

Design Is In The Details

Pool safety is an important detail. An automatic pool cover is located under the coping and an automated key opens and closes the pool cover. An arching pool jet is located in the travertine paving.

Paving details add interest to the integrity of the job.

An antique iron trellis planted with a flowering vine softens a blank wall.

An outdoor shower adds interest and function to the wall of this pool house.

Contractors and Design Resources

Contractors

Empire Construction
General Contractors Sacramento
(530) 795-1132
gregchar@sbcglobal.net

Green Future
Landscape Contractor
(916) 967-1250
C.EMMONS@comcast.net

CLK Construction
Cortlandt Koerwitz
CLKconstruction.com
cort@winfirst.com

Matt Haseltine Landscaping
(530)756-2042

Design Resources

Outdoor Lighting:
Valley Lighting Company
Mark Miyamoto
ValleyLightingCompany.com
mark@valleylightingcompany.com

Lighting:
FX Luminaire
Low voltage lighting
http.www.fxl.com

Interior Design:
Tammy Isaak
(916) 483-2483
cell (916) 796-5620
Tammy@studioredinteriors.com

Mosaic Artists:
Dylan Tellesen
2315 Fern Ave.
Chico, CA 95926

Robin Indar
home (530) 891-7915
cell (530) 321-2602
robinindar@yahoo.com

Fountains:
Pottery World
4419 Granite Dr.
Rocklin, CA 95677
(916) 624-8080
www.potteryworld.com

Flora Tropicana
10255 Grant Line Rd.
Elk Grove, CA 95624
(916) 714-4200
www.floratropicana.com

Haddonstone (USA) Ltd.
201 Heller Place
Bellmawr, NJ 08031
(856) 931-7011
fax: (856) 931-0040
www.haddonstone.com

Prefab Outdoor Fireplaces:
Designs By Gary, Inc.
(949) 581-1919
www.exteriorfireplaces.com

Outdoor Kitchens:
Diablo Grills Outdoor Kitchen
Sacramento, CA 95827
(916) 361-7100
www.DiabloGrills.com

Building Materials:
Silverado Masonry Design Center
Liz Serven
Sacramento, CA 95826
 (916) 381-8711; (916) 769-0879
www.silveradoonline.com

Synthetic Grass:
Turf Grass
Paul and Annie Costa
(530) 432-5836
www.TuffGrass.com

Outdoor Furniture/Garden Ornamentation:
AHFA- American Home
Furnishings Alliance
contact: Jackie Hirschhaut
(336) 884-5000 ext. 116
www.findyourfurniture.com

North of South
545 Laurel Street
Petaluma, CA 94952
(707) 484-8294
www.North-of-South.com

Casual Elements
2419 Mercantile Drive Suite B
Rancho Cordova, CA 95742
(916) 853-2210
www.casual-elements.com

Pottery World
4419 Granite Dr.
Rocklin, CA 95677
(916) 624-8080
www.potteryworld.com

Specialty Nurseries:
Green Acres Nursery
8501 Jackson Rd.
Sacramento, CA 95826
(916) 381-1625

Fair Oaks Nursery
4681 Fair Oaks Blvd.
Sacramento, CA 95864
(916) 483-1830

High Hand Nursery
3750 Taylor Rd.
Loomis, CA 95650

Natural Stone Veneer:
Montana Rockworks Inc.
1107 Rose Crossing
Kallispell, MT 59901
(406) 752-7625
fax: (406) 752-7645
www.montanarockworks.com

Hand Carved Granite:
Stone Forest
(505) 986-8883
fax: (505) 982-2712
www.stoneforest.com

low maintenance
low H$_2$O
drip irrigation
raised planters for elderly
rocks / stone (blue)
seating

firepit
blue glass - gurgles
blue pottery